Rainbow Mirrors

Poems on Love, Life and Dreams Coming True

SMARA

INDIA · SINGAPORE · MALAYSIA

ISBN 979-8-88749-973-4

Illustrations by Artist Prikesh Ravi
Inspiration by Shantha Ram

Rainbow Mirrors

In this collection of poems is woven a story of love, life, finding one's self and dreams coming true.

Read from the beginning, it will take you on a journey till the end.

We will meet in the poems you resonate with.

Contents

PART 4. SEEING YOU WITHIN AND WITHOUT – IN ALL EXISTENCE AROUND

PART 5. THE RENDEZVOUS – SOME DREAMS; SOME TRUE

Part 1

∼

The Flip

Meeting you for the first time in this life time

---

*If your beloved has the life of a fire, step
in now and burn along.*

Rumi

01
Today I am Born

—

World knows of a mother's pain
What about the cries of the new born?
Maybe it cries because it is darker outside.

Why did I get lost in this sea?
What purpose did I see?

I Kept waddling, trying to reach the shores;
I kept running, trying to see another soul;
I kept counting, my days grew more and more;
I kept waiting, my pain was now making me whole.

In the spheres of my pain,
I found a cradle for my nights.
One dark night I was deep asleep.

See! there is light!! My heart nudged me awake!

"No lights enter this shrouded place" – I sighed.
It is a fire, told my quivering heart in awe.

I gazed into this lightlets nest!
It was his burning eyes.

The fire was in sight.
It was darkly bright and beautiful;
It was tall and all and bountiful;
I looked at it with awe, what majesty in display!

The blazing fire gazed at me fair and straight.
Do I bow before it or should I wait?

I was beckoned to come closer and so I went.
It gripped me with its blanching tongues,
I was frozen. It crushed me, burnt me,
twisted and turned me.

" Are you afraid?" It stared at me;
" No, I am coming alive." I stared back at it.
It took me again, I was battered and shattered,
Till the last drop in me fell away and scattered.

"Are you still holding?" It mocked.
" Are you the sun?" I asked.
"No! I am his!" – It let me see.
And then I saw the most magnificent scene!

A man and his fire in a fiery commune.
Oh, all the light is here, I see!!
How could all this fire inside one man be?

Today I am born. I bow before thee.
You ignited the flame in me.

02
You Are...

—

You are...

      The twinkle in the stars;
      The state of all the arts.
      The space within a nest;
      Streams of twilight from the west.

You are...

      The first thought in my mornings
      The last thought of my nights
      And everything else in between
      these times.

You are...

> The music in the heart beats-
> Carrying the whispers unheard.
> The flutter of a butterfly's wing-
> Setting up hurricanes in my world.

03

In the Field Beyond Right and Wrong

—

Taking a leap into horizons unclear;
Shedding layers that were all once dear;
A tiny voice, a flickering flame-
Awaiting within all these years.

The path and me – is it my lone destiny?
What if I fail; What if I am lost?
These penalties are illusory to last.
I am breaking free from the dualities cast.

Venturing beyond right and wrong,
Catching up to myself somewhere along.
"What I seek is also seeking me,"
Gratitudes to Rumi for teaching me.

In the quest of a happy ending,
I find new beginnings staring at me.

Am I taking this path or the path is taking me?
Along the way can I co-create my destiny?

The universe creating infinity itself;
The multiverse within me cannot be any less.

A perennial seeking-a tempest in making;
This search will be on even when I am gone.

Will I see you some day in the field beyond right and
wrong?

Part 2

The Journey Without

In your light I learn how to love.
In your beauty, how to make poems.
You dance inside my chest where no one sees you, but sometimes
I do, and that sight becomes this art.

Rumi

04
My Heart

—

My heart is a slide;
My heart is a swing;
A merry go round-
More merrier; Less bound.

Some days it is a friend,
Keeping up with my trends;
Other days becomes a foe,
Suddenly turning dense.

Some days it flows freely like a river;
Other days a mirage that soon disappears.

Some days it is open, then comes the rains.
Some days it is closed, clouded by my pains.

Sometimes it is silent; sometimes it stings.
Somedays When I am alone,
It sits next to me and sings.

Some days it is broke, waiting to be stoked.
Somedays it is lost; Not wanting to be probed.

Some days it storms-a howling gale;
But storms clear paths, removing all stale.

Somedays it is this; Somedays it is that;
But always it keeps calling
your name from its depths..

My heart is a slide; My heart is a swing.
My heart is a merry go round –
More merrier when you are around..

05
A Billion Butterflies
—

I am a person – so much alive.
I live every moment again and again.
What do I do if my heart is a magnifier?

Do I make myself a lesser me,
Or is it okay to just let it be?

A universe within is holding me;
It reflects you in all its beams.
Someday I will tell you what it means.

I am carrying this sack with me,
I collect moments to fill my sack.
These are the moments that hold my back.

Some moments tinged with pain;
Some are poignant and slain.
Some are extravagant with love;
Some I don't know how.

Some echoes with your laughter,
Some laced with tears.
Some silent with promises,
Some vibrant, when you were near.

Some vivid with colours,
Some filled with your scent;
Some carrying our dreams,
Some lost in my depths.

I want my sack filled with these moments-
One day till it bursts. How do I want to die?
Bursting into a billion butterflies-
Flying towards you carrying pieces of the sky…

06
Codes

A connection,
An infinite affection,
As spontaneous as an elemental reaction;
More powerful than a nuclear emission.

You opened the door to the depths of my soul.
A forgotten code gets activated deep within the core.
The DNAs start to unwind as they are not stranded any more.

Beyond Darwin's tracings,
Under Newton's musings,
Within Pascal's units,
Without Einstein's constant,
Inside the earth's animus,
Outside the universe's dark matter-

One thing is the same:
It has but no name.
When the lost dreamer awakens,
The world is not the same.

The only place for singularity
in the universe is a black hole.
I have come so far,
I was dreaming of going home.
When I looked into your eyes,
I found I was not lost anymore.

Tao cherishes the empty space.
It says "Be by not being"
To love and to live–
Can you do so by not doing?
Can you be by not being?
If I answer, "I don't know",
Then does it mean-
I know by not knowing??

07

Let Yesterdays Be...

—

A dawn with lazy dews.
Grasses sway looking anew.
When light rays enters a dwindling dew,
Rainbows spring to life looking for you!

Happy birds chirping with zest,
Crows too start singing their best.
A prayer song from far away,
A peaceful melody coming your way!

Let yesterdays be;
Leave tomorrows free.
At this moment you are here;
Do you realize you are so dear!?

Alone you are not;
A part of this world.
Its beauties with its beasts,
It is all for you; You are all for it.

Inside little moments
Are hidden life's treasures.
If you find a way to find them every day,
Then the beasts go ablaze,
And the beauty takes its place!

Part 3

The Journey Within

_The wound is the place where the
light enters you_

Rumi

08

In Search of the "W"

—

A hole inside me! How could it be?
I pondered and grieved.
My heart wandered with me.
It told me all stories to bring me reason.

I want not a reason, I said.
Let's anyway take a look – it nudged.
As we looked within its darkest depths,
A shudder passed through our breaths.

It is not a hole. It is a black nest!
In it breeds a beast, its silent stealthy self.
It beats with my beats, heaves with my sighs and smiles
in my cries.
The black nest concealed at its best.

It wasn't just me as I had thought.
There is this beast inside my heart!
I am looking at it, I am scared;
But it doesn't seem to care.

Alas if I had known how deep its roots will plod me;
How sunk its nails will pierce me;
Oh! How could this be part of me?

" STOP WHINING!" it roared.
A roar that could shatter heaven
and hells' doors.
" GO FIND YOURSELF!"
It pushed me, stamped me and tossed me out.
I fell limp; I got up to fight.
Stood facing it straight.
The beast was impatient with me.
How could it be? An indignation to me!

And so against my beast,
I started the battle; Went on full throttle;
It went on for years.
I was never less fierce.

The scars and the aches made me so aged.

I wished it would end; I was weary and glazed.

I sat down to catch my breath; The beast sat next to me.

It looked at me with anger;

I couldn't bear it any longer.

I am so alone, you took everything from me.

Why am I still fighting when all I want is to leave?

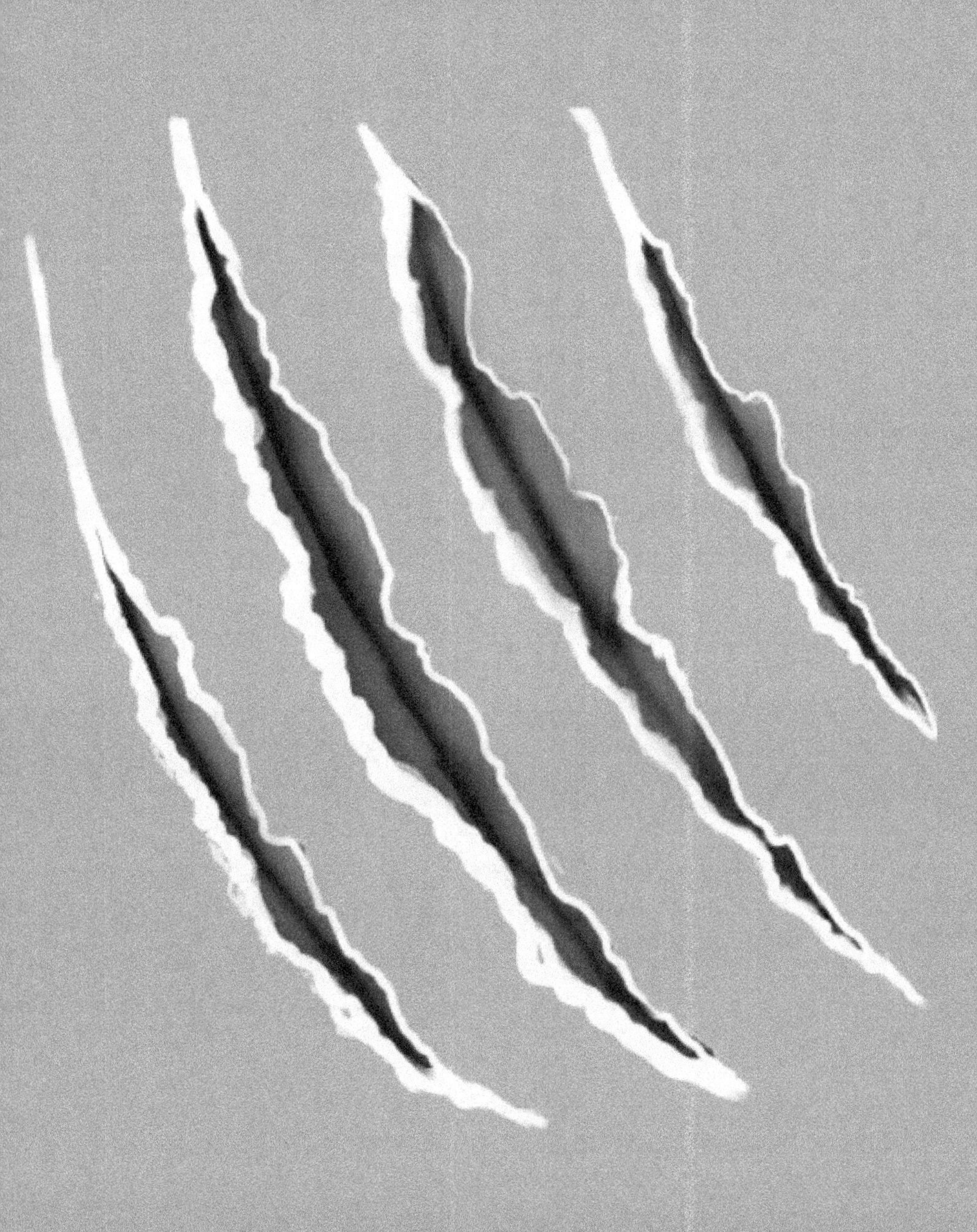

"OH!!! DON'T BLAME ME!" it laughed aloud and
roared:

I AM NOT YOUR BATTLE;
I AM YOUR SHADOW SIDE.

I AM FILLING YOUR HOLE!
I AM MAKING YOU WHOLE.

NOW GO FIND YOUR RIGHT FIGHTS,
YOU ARE YOUR LIGHT!"

It pushed me, stamped me and tossed me out.

I fell limp but got back up to fight.

This time, the beast and me-on the same side.

I have learnt my lesson,

Now there is no fright.

When I own my darkness I shine more bright!

09
Wings of Fire

—

Lulled into life's stifling travesties,
I trudge through the days,
Dream through the nights,
Looking for meaning along my ways.

My sorrows are the seas.
The mountains are my glees.
In the sand dunes of the desserts,
Are fossiled all my efforts.

An arduous path; A murderous sail.
My destiny and me! What is more to see?
Without you by my side, will I survive this sea?

A frenzied fire rummages through me;
The craters running deeper are neither kinder to me.
My path is strewn with tests, I am trying my best!

And then my fire whispered to me,
" Wake up oh wanderer!
Don't get swayed.
I burn high when you forget your wings.

Mountains in your path,
Don't get shackled and chained.
Oceans of pain,
Don't swallow in vain.

This parody is all the same.
It is meant for all the lame.

You may choose to enter this maze,
Or simply fly over the haze.
For your wings are of fire,
That which can never tire.

10

Twinkle Twinkle Little Star

—

A star is nesting in its nebula;
A fire blazing in its core.
Swallowed in its own gravity,
But not a black hole.

Fissions and fusions,
Its atoms are sealing;
In its core it is healing.
It cannot be dwarfed;
It cannot be stopped.
It is unbound by the immensity of the space,
Measuring infinity with its own light rays.

It spirals in a supernova,
Questions itself – "Will I explode?"
When at last it reaches the depths,
It is unsure whether it is still alive or dead.

It twinkles with delight,
When it comes to realize:
Fires cannot scorch a star!
It has made it this far.

It starts to dazzle bright,
And dabble colours to the night.
To send out light,
And show its might.

Twinkle twinkle little star
How I wonder what you are!
How I wonder what you are!

11
Finding Space
—

Love pulls the soul to where it belongs.
It sees no conditions; It knows no laws.
Sometimes the load is too much to behold;
Parts of me break; Parts of me hold.

The broken pieces are floating by;
The pieces holding persevere to try.
Rumi says, "The heart will keep breaking
Until it opens."
Someday I will thank you for teaching me these portions.

Between the love and the heart breaks,
There is a quiet inner space.
It is full of love and it is seems to be safe.
I will wait for you there till it's time again to see your
lovely face.

12

A Personal Apocalypse

—

Sun stands mighty blazing in the skies.
There is a mightier sun inside our minds.

It gets darker at times.
The pettiness around may cloud our sight.
But the sun inside never sets.
Let its light pierce our depths.

The path is blurry,
But there is no hurry.
We have waited so long,
Now the winters are gone.

A personal Apocalypse;
Facing the shadows in its chalice.
We have seen it all,
It is time to see beyond.
We will decipher the music,
Amidst the chaos and noise.

Let the rains dissolve the clouds – both within and
without;
Love can wash away all our doubts.
Sun shines across a spotless mind;
One day we will remember
We are beings of light.

Part 4

~

Seeing You Within and Without – in All Existence Around

I am in you and I am you.
No one can understand this until he has lost his mind.

Rumi

13
Only You
—

In you I see my universe;
In this universe I see only you.

14

Once Again Today

—

My heart suddenly skipped a beat.
I saw a million flowers blossoming;
What is it? I was swept away.

Oh! it is your Lovely face,
You took my breath away.
Once again today 😊

15

More Lovers on Earth

—

The world with its share of dread & dark,
Is also the place where my person walks.
Can I lessen the darkness,
Can I light up the path?

An act of kindness, a show of strength,
A pint of hope, an inch of zest.
I know these are small to even the odds;
But I can't keep waiting for the gods.

Drop by drop I will add.
(No, I ain't mad!)
World someday will not be dim,
It will become more worthy of him.

How can a drop deepen the ocean? – you may ask.
If all the drops thought so,
where would all the oceans go?

I will keep adding the little I could;
Day by day, in some way,
I will make this world a brighter place;
For this is also my person's space.

If only there were more lovers on earth,
World wouldn't be in such a haste.
There would be more beauty to gaze.

16

A Star is Born

—

A shooting star,
A million splendid hues,
A lightlets nest,
A rainbow at its dazzling best-
All together shines not as bright as you.

You have come to touch more lives
And spread more smiles,
Soaring high beyond the miles.
Love yourself – a star is born.
Happy birthday to the one still unborn.

17
Danke
—

Human body has octillion atoms.
With you in the nucleus of every atom,
The wandering electrons gathered around;
The lost harmony was again found.

"A gazillion electrons revolving around an octillion thee;
Inside every atom in the universe in me.
The scattered teslas now a focussed beam;
Danke Lieber geliebte (thank you dear beloved!)
Resonates the quantas in me."

Part 5

The Rendezvous –
Some Dreams; Some True

*The minute I heard my first love story, I started looking for
you, not knowing how blind that was. Lovers don't finally meet
somewhere. They are in each other all along.*

Rumi

18
The Pull

—

I was looking for you between the raindrops.
Some days I saw you too, were you really there?

In the trees and the leaves,
Sky and the clouds,
I see your tinge in all existence around.

I called out to you from the mountain tops,
You struck me as lightning and seized all my thoughts.
I ran till the horizons; my heart stopped out of breath.
You coursed through me as a gulp of air and took me
back from death.

The oceans and the riverbeds
have seen me roam by.
They know my stories;
They know my cries.
They sing to me and whisper your name,
Trying to stop me from going insane.

Sometimes I think of going into the sea;
What if you are within and I fail to see.
I then hear you calling me from behind.
I step back and turn around,
But You are not to be found.

The silences between the sounds,
And the emptiness between the clouds,
Carry the messages from your end.
They have become my only friends.

One fine day life was its usual pace.
I saw you this time face to face.
The sky came down very near,
The ground beneath me disappeared.

My heart didn't just skip a beat,
It skipped a whole symphony.

Dimensions froze; Timelines closed
How come today you are so near!?
Is this another dream or is it for real?!

An encounter beyond worlds;
An oneness beyond words.

I looked at you and I saw,
All along you were not afar.
You were right within inside my heart;
With every beat, you were guiding me:
Tugging me here, pulling me there,
To travel this far and here you are.

The pull.

19
Dreams Come True

—

Sometimes dreams slide down into reality;
When you hold my hands, do you know you are holding
my dream...

20

Rainbow Mirrors

When drops of tears fall from my eyes,
I think of your smile; It is my ray of sunshine.
It pierces the drops; Suddenly rainbows pop!

Rainbow mirrors glitter in the skies;
Purple pink horizons reflect your smiles.

You are all the colours; I am all your shades.
I come to realize that life's promise won't fade.

21
Iris Tales

—

I don't know the colour of your eyes!
Every time I looked into them,
I got so lost,
Forgot who I was
Or what I came to see.

22
When I See You
—

When I see your smile,
When I see your face,
When tiny little details of you
Start filling my gaze,

My eyes ignite my heart;
My heart sets fire to the soul;
My soul lights up the mind;
Meanwhile my body comes alive.

Across all dimensions I Am on fire.

How do you do this every time?
Keeping me calm, turning me on
all at the same time!

23
Lost and Found

Our real conversations unfold
when we are in our space;
Out of words,
Out of thoughts,
Out of this world,
We find the most meaning
when we are lost in our embrace.

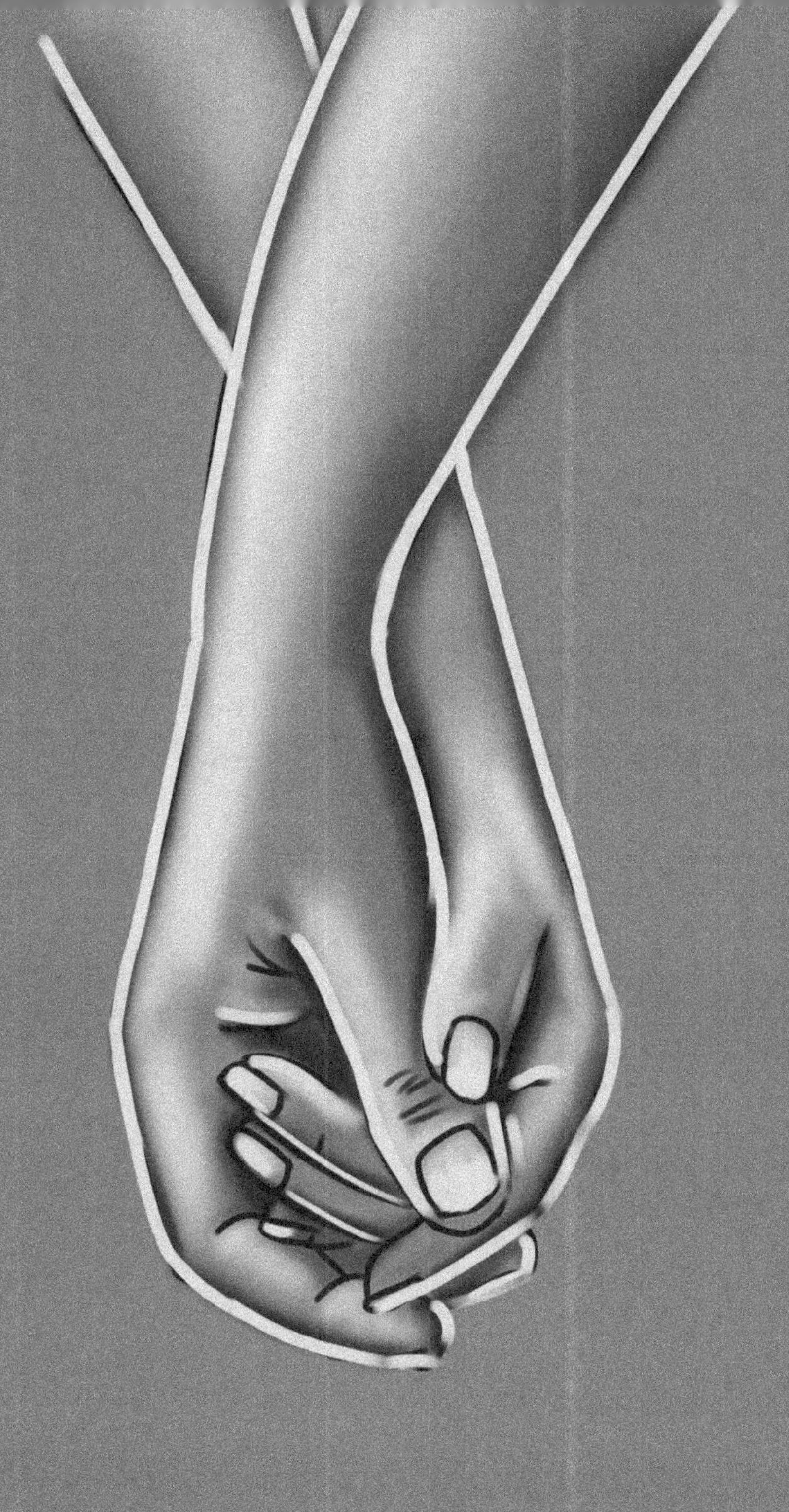

24
The End

—

You are beyond a name, beyond the form;
You are the very force behind all forms.

You are the light in which I get lost;
And also the darkness where I find myself at last.

You are everything and the nothing that holds it all;
You are the infinity and also the void.

You are my beginning;
In You I end.

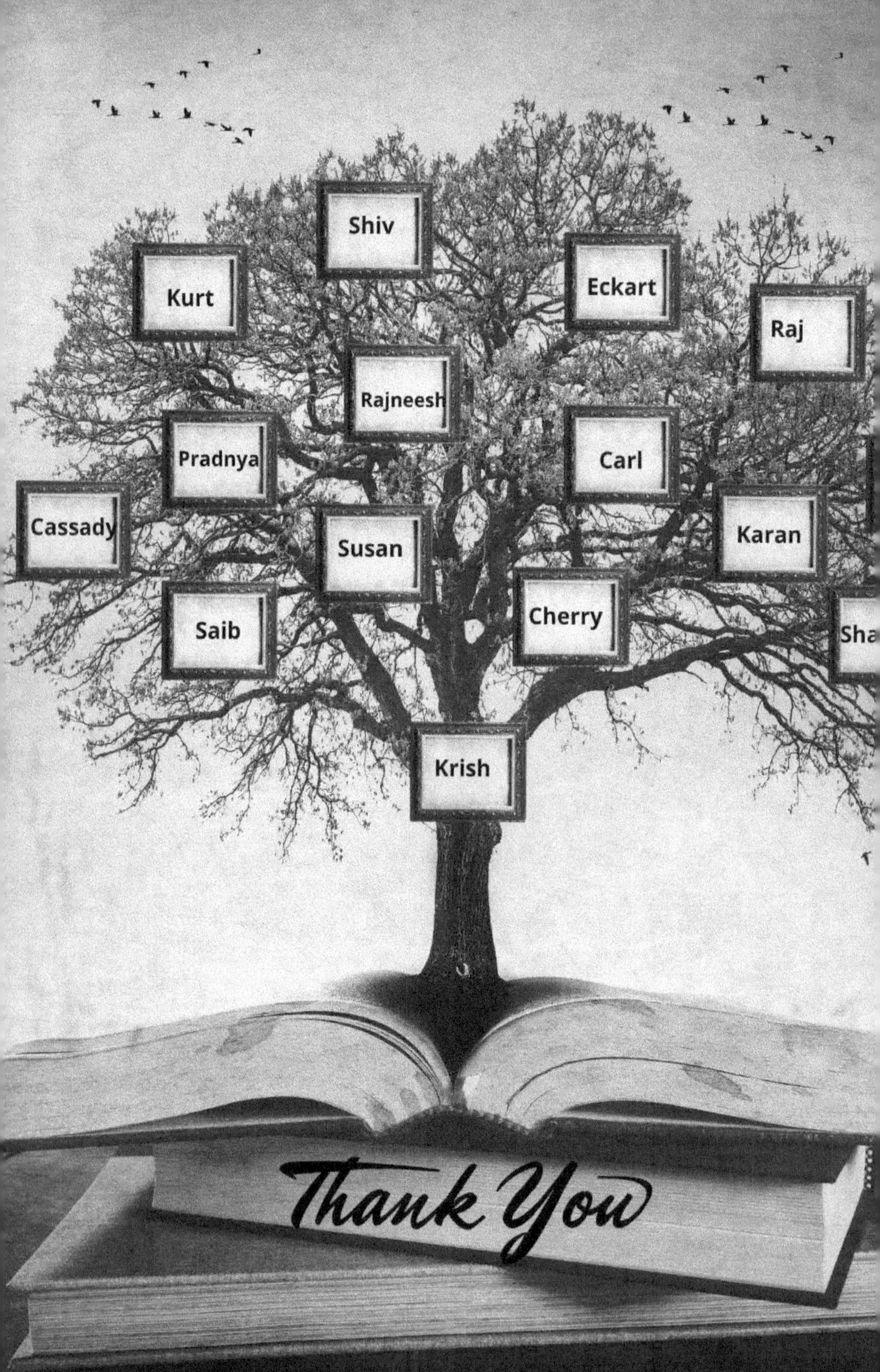

Shiv
Kurt
Eckart
Raj
Rajneesh
Pradnya
Carl
Cassady
Karan
Susan
Saib
Cherry
Sha
Krish
Thank You